Jasper Johns

Leo Steinberg

Jasper Johns

George Wittenborn, Inc., New York 21 N. Y.

This monograph is an enlarged and revised edition of the article which was originally published in Metro, International Magazine of Contemporary Art, 4/5, May, 1962. Milan.

64-34

6

December 1961. Johns is exhibiting four gray paintings, recently finished. One of them is a sketch — encaustic and sculpmetal on paper; but it made its point so well that there seemed no need for elaborate execution. The picture displays, on a square field, Johns's characteristic dense veil of graded gray strokes: paint that denotes nothing but painting. Hinged to the top of the square is a woodblock; and four raised letters on it which we see in a murky rectangular field, like a reflection in water, illegibly, upside down. But the block has left a fair imprint directly below, on the painting itself. It spells LIAR. Does it mean anything?

It need not. It's a device for printing an indispensable word. Or just Painting with a bit of Dada provocation on top (but we are too sly to be had by a four-letter word). Or it's an allegory concerning the hinges that hold life to art. For the woodblock, existing in actual space, is real, a piece out of life, hence illegible, topsy-turvy. Yet it is this that imprints itself on the painted field, where it is set right to become perfectly clear; such being the Revelations of Art. Life's murky message is decoded by Art, and there it is, spelling LIAR — the word cleared of every accretion of passion, a forgotten name plate that's been there since long before we moved in.

The word moves out into the room and hangs there like a frozen voice, waiting to thaw and settle. On whom? On what? Which side of the fence? Does it mean anything?

To whom? To the schoolboy learning to read? To posterity? To the painter who made it? His friends?

To the same painter who's moved on to make something else? To the critic who already knows what « the needs of art » are and who can see that they will not be served by this sort of picture? To us when we see an implacable presence and a gaping metaphor generated by crude literal means?

The elements of Johns's picture lie side by side like flint pebbles. Rubbed together they would spark a flame, and that is their meaning perhaps. But Johns does not claim to have ever heard of the invention of fire. He just finds and places the pebbles.

His Critics

He had his first one-man show four years ago, exhibiting the now famous variations on the American flag, on targets, numbers and letters. Also included were:

Book (1957), an actual book spread open, then overpainted in wax, red pages, yellow edges, blue binding — a paralyzed book in a boxed frame;

Newspaper (1957), encaustic and newsprint on canvas;

Canvas (1957), an all-gray painting in which a small canvas had been glued face down to a larger one;

Drawer (1957), all-gray again, with the front panel of a plain two-knobbed drawer inserted just below center.

The pictures aroused both enthusiasm and consternation, above all by their subjects. These were of such unprecedented « banality », it seemed nothing so humdrum had been seen since the other day, or since Art began.
Why had he chosen to paint subjects of such aggressive uninterest?
To be different?

The validity of this answer depends on its tone. When you hear it said with a shrug, explain to the speaker that he has no point at all; we simply restate our question: « Why, if he wanted to be different, did he choose to be different in this and no other manner? ».
But that same answer, made in goodwill, can describe a crucial problem in a young artist's development. For becoming a painter is like groping one's way out of a cluttered room in the dark. Beginning to walk, he tumbles over another man's couch, changes course to collide with someone's commode, then butts against a work table that can't be disturbed. Everything has its use and its user, and no need of him. When Johns was discharged from the army in 1952 and settled down in New York (he was no longer « going to be a painter », the time having come to start being one), he began to make small abstract collages from paper scraps. Being told that they looked like those of Kurt Schwitters, he went to look at Schwitters' collages and found that they did look like his own. He was trespassing, and he veered away — to be different.

The subject matter he displayed in January 1958 was different enough to precipitate a crisis in criticism. Despite a half century of formalist indoctrination, it proved almost impossible to see the paintings for subject matter. *Art News*, flying Johns's *Target with Faces* on its January 1958 cover, labeled it « neo-Dada » — and the word untied every tongue. People who might have wondered what to say about Johns could thenceforth recite whatever they remembered having read about Dada (*). It remained the most interesting point about Johns that he managed somehow to discover uninteresting subjects. Critics could discuss Johns's work with keen political sense and a minimum of actual looking. Harold Rosenberg credited Johns with sneering at Philistine values (« The Audience as Subject »; catalogue introduction for a show in Houston, Texas, Nov. 1959). Johns's flag is « obviously intended as provocation. Instead of concentrating on art, its problems and its needs, the artist speaks to the audience about itself... Johns sticks right up against the gallery goer's nose the emblem he adores ».
Hilton Kramer proclaimed the reverse: « His designs are mock-naive. His hand-painted American flags, targets,

numbers, and so on, are a kind of Grandma Moses version of Dada. But... Dada sought to repudiate and criticize bourgeois values, whereas Johns, like Rauschenberg, aims to please and confirm the decadent periphery of bourgeois taste ». (*ARTS*, Feb. 1959, p. 49).

Critics who looked longer at the paintings themselves also arrived at opposite conclusions concerning the role of the subjects. Fairfield Porter (he and Robert Rosenblum were the first writers to acclaim Johns's work) thought that the paintings had to do with a way of seeing. « He looks for the first time, like a child, at things that have no meaning to the child, yet, or necessarily ». (*Art News*, Jan. 1958, p. 20. — Yet Johns's regard for the right shape and order of numbers is not characteristic of one who knows not the meaning of what he transcribes).
Rosenblum wrote: « Johns first astonishes the spectator and then obliges him to examine for the first time the visual qualities of a humdrum object he had never before paused to look at ». (*Art International*, Sept. 1960, p. 75. — But if Johns worked with a spectator in mind, is it likely that he addressed himself by preference to those who never pause to look at such things as letters?).
And John B. Myers, calling Johns « the Surrealist of naming things », wrote: « Like the small child who holds up an egg, having discovered such an object for the first time in a hidden nest, and cries " Egg! " — so Johns has made clear what things *are*... » (*Evergreen Review*, March-April 1960, p. 78. — But what child holds his breath crying « Egg! » for a year — the time it took Johns to complete his *Gray Alphabets* of 1956?).
To see it, to show it, to name it — these are three motives here imputed to Johns in his choice of commonplace themes. The three authors agree that the chief event in a Johns painting is to render an overlooked subject suddenly recognized.

Another group of critics concluded that Johns chose his subjects to make them disappear altogether. « Johns likes to paint objects so familiar that the spectator can cease to think about them and concentrate on the poetic qual-

(*) *Newsweek's* sole editorial comment (March 31, 1958): « Dada, it seems, rides again ». *Time* (May 4, 1959), in a piece entitled « His heart belongs to Dada », explained: « Like Johns, the Dadaists deliberately tried to strip art of all sentiment and all significance ». Michel Ragon, reporting on American art in *Cimaise* (Jan. 1959, p. 28) wrote: « Jasper Johns est une explosion dadaïste un peu comparable à Yves Klein à Paris ». Pierre Schneider, reporting in *Art News* (March 1959, p. 48) on Johns's first show in Paris, observed that the subjects were « alienated from their meaning by being represented in an unctuous " painterly " manner. It is a sign of the times: Dada, like everybody else, has gone to art school ». « Dada's the Disease », diagnosed Emily Genauer and informed readers of the N.Y. *Herald Tribune* (April 3, 1960) that Johns « likes to attach empty coke bottles to his canvas » — a mistaken reference to a painting by Rauschenberg.

ities of the picture itself » (*). Which is exactly what Ortega y Gasset used to write of Velázquez — that his vulgar themes, such as court fools, were designed « to force the public to focus its attention on the art of painting and to give less importance to its subjects ». May we point out that in their alleged roles as promoters of art appreciation both Johns and Velázquez are failures? The latter because the sorry stare of his dwarfs is as unforgettable as his palette; and Johns, because similarly none of his subjects ever succeeds in getting itself overlooked. On the contrary.

We thus have a critical situation in which some believe that the subjects were chosen to make them more visible, others, that they were chosen to become invisible. It is the sort of contradiction that becomes a heuristic event. It sends you back to the paintings with a more potent question: What in the work, you ask, elicits such contrariety? It then turns out that the work is such as to make both groups of critics — wrong as they were — right. For Johns's pictures are situations wherein the subjects are constantly found and lost, seen and ignored, submerged and recovered again. He has regained that perpetual oscillation which characterized our looking at pre-abstract art. But whereas, in traditional art, the oscillation was between the painted surface and the subject in depth, Johns succeeds in making the pendulum swing within the post-Cubist flatland of modern art. But the habit of dissociating « pure painting » from content is so ingrained, that almost no critic was able to see both together (**).

Johns has built himself a composite language in which paint and words, objects and emblems converge in a single image-meaning. Subject matter is back not as an adulteration, nor as a concession, nor in some sort of partnership, but as the very condition of painting, wherein content and form, life and art, the paint and the message are so much one and the same, that the distinction is not yet, or no longer intelligible.
This amazing result is largely a function of his original subjects. I want to question these subjects for their common character and see how they work for him in his paintings. If I can get some of these questions answered, I may no longer need to ask what Johns's intentions were in choosing to paint flags, targets, numbers, etc.

THE SUBJECTS

The subjects which Jasper Johns chose to paint up to 1958, the year of his first public showing, have these points in common:
1. Whether objects or signs, they are man-made things.
2. All are commonplaces of our environment.

3

10

(*) *Charm*, April 1959, p. 85. Cf. Ben Heller in *School of New York: Some Younger Artists*, ed. by B. H. Friedman, Grove Press, New York 1959: « Primarily, their importance is less as flags or targets than as means of forcing the viewer to focus upon the canvas itself, to react to it as an immediate and direct painting experience ». And William Rubin in « Younger American Painters », *Art International*, Vol. IV, No. 1, 1960: « For Johns the image is meaningful in its meaninglessness ».
(**) The exception is Robert Rosenblum, who responded at once to a « visual and intellectual impact ». Johns's work, he wrote, « assaults and enlivens the mind and the eye with the exhilaration of discovery ». Thus in *ARTS*, Jan. 1958, p. 54. And again in *Art International*, Sept. 1960, p. 77: « In general, Johns establishes a spare and taut equilibrium of few visual elements whose immediate sensuous impact is as compelling as the intellectual jolt... ».

3. All possess a ritual or conventional shape. Not to be altered.
4. They are either whole entities or complete systems.
5. They tend to prescribe the picture's shape and dimensions.
6. They are flat.
7. They tend to be non-hierarchic, permitting Johns to maintain a pictorial field of leveled equality, without points of stress or privilege.
8. They are associable with sufferance rather than action.

I discuss each of these eight in turn.

1. **That Johns's subjects are man-made objects or signs** is apparent. The fact that they are man-made means that they are, in fact, makable. And this is the liberating discovery for the painter whose mind is both literal and contemporary: the man-made alone can be made, whereas everything else that's to be seen in our environment is only imitable by make-believe. The position of esthetic anti-illusionism finds here its logical resting place. The street and the sky — they can only be simulated on canvas; but a flag, a target, a 7 — these can be made, and the completed painting will represent no more than what it actually is. For no likeness or image of a 7 is paintable, only the thing itself.
A crucial problem of 20th century art — how to make the painting a firsthand reality — resolves itself when the subject matter shifts from nature to culture.

2. **The subjects are commonplaces of our environment.** So worded, Johns's preference would place him with Caravaggio, Courbet, or the American Ashcan School painters, all artists who chose lowly themes. But Johns doesn't give us the commonplace *in* a painting (transfigured by light, composition and style), but the commonplace *as* a painting. This is different.
The choice of the commonplace does not necessarily follow from the decision to paint only man-made things: he might have chosen to paint the groundplan of the Taj Mahal. What he does choose is always a Universal: his *Coat Hanger*, for instance. It is not made of wood, which would have placed it at a particular level of price and quality; nor of some shiny plastic which would grade it on a scale of modernity. His wire hanger is of the kind nobody buys or selects — it comes free of charge from the cleaner; an object that enters everyman's house and is discarded at every back door. Similarly, his *Book*, *Newspaper*, *Hook* (1958) and flags are, despite their concreteness, as impartial, as classless and universal as the primary numbers are, or the alphabet.

His subjects are indeed commonplace, but no more « banal » than unpeeled potatoes or unrationed air.

Why did he choose them?

A young woman wrote to me in June 1960: « When I saw Jasper Johns's paintings I wondered why he wasted those beautiful Chardin-like whites and greys on flags and numbers ». It was the classic feminine disapproval — like the familiar « I-don't-know-what-he-sees-in-her! » — of a man's love that seems misdirected. And yet, so far only Rosenblum has remarked that there is a factor of love in the way Johns works with his subjects.
But love is a busy word. Perhaps the sniper who has picked his quarry from a line of uniformed enemy soldiers does the same thing. It is a matter of getting the object in focus, until it is not even one of its kind, but absolutely alone. Changing the object by a change of attitude, the only way it can be changed without violation.

Recently Pierre Restany (*Cimaise*, Sept. 1961) has written that Johns's essential gesture as a painter is to bestow uniqueness on the commonplace.

What happens when we see a painted commonplace by Jasper Johns? I do not believe that we experience a revelation about the design and shape of flag or target. Nor that we lose the subject in the delight of pure painting. But in observing these standardized things we sense an unfamiliar deceleration of their normal rate of existence. The flag stiffens, is slowly hand-painted, and — as the end stage of a process that began with the stop of its flutter — cast in bronze. The Stars and Stripes forever.

All of them are slowed down. As they were not spawned in the outpouring of industry, so they no longer submit to the mechanical gestures of human users — the flipping of pages, the saluting of flags, opening of a drawer, computing of numbers, etc. What we see when we face a Johns commonplace is the possibility of a changed attitude; better still, the possibility of an object's lone self-existence without any human attitude whatsoever surrounding it. What Johns loves in his objects is that they are nobody's preference; not even his own. By a strange paradox, these hand-made, uniquely made commonplace things, are relieved of man's shadow.

If his works are disturbing at all, perhaps it is because they insinuate our own absence, not from a scene of romantic desolation, nor from a universe of abstract energies, but from our bedroom and kitchen.

3. A Johns subject possesses a respected ritual or conventional shape.

It is never enough to say that he paints numbers; add that he paints them in proper order (i.e. not in childlike, or ignorant, or esthetic disregard of their meaning). Add that his alphabets run A to Z, and that a ruler used in his paintings is always left whole and straight, i.e. not creatively rearranged. Picabia in 1918 had incorporated a tape measure in a picture called *Les Centimètres*; but the tape had been broken and stuck down in pieces. The Cubists used to make it a practice to disrespect the true count of things: put three strings on a guitar, four or six lines on a stave of sheet music. Such departure from given facts was felt to be a token of their transfiguration; it symbolized their enlistment by art. Byzantine architects sometimes ornamented a church facade with fragments of antique inscriptions, some of them upside down. The inversion, whether willful or ignorant, was an index of alienation from the antique literary tradition. And 20th century art has continually made use of common objects, including numbers and clusters of letters, but modified, or freely fragmented, and in surprised combinations.

In Jasper Johns, the conventional meaning is never flouted. No personal attitude of anger, irony or estheticism alters the shapes he transcribes. Nothing recalls the waywardness, the irreverence, or the untidiness of most original Dada productions. In all his subjects, Johns recognizes a prefixed form which he accepts much as artists formerly accepted the anatomy of the body. This had its practical side. « Using the design of the American flag took care of a great deal for me because I didn't have to design it », he once said. (Which reminds one that the best story tellers, such as Homer and Shakespeare, did not, like O. Henry or Somerset Maugham, invent their own plots). « So I went on to similar things like the targets », Johns continued, « — things the mind already knows. That gave me room to work on other levels ». It is as though Johns had decided to draw on both modes of non-representational painting — Geometric Abstraction and Abstract Expressionism, though their common tendency is to exclude one another. His way of realizing his subjects permits him to submit to an impersonal discipline of ruled lines, while still responding to every painterly impulse. And Johns succeeded in uniting these two disparate ways of art with yet a third, which is normally antithetical to them both; the most literal realism. It's the way things are that is the proper subject for art.

When you ask Johns why he did this or that in a painting, he answers so as to clear himself of responsibility. A given decision was made for him by the way things are, or was suggested by an accident he never invited.

Regarding the four casts of faces he placed in four oblong boxes over one of the targets:
Q: *Why did you cut them off just under the eyes?*
A: *They wouldn't have fitted into the boxes if I'd left them whole.*

He was asked why his bronze sculpture of an electric bulb was broken up into bulb, socket and cord:
A: *Because, when the parts came back from the foundry, the bulb wouldn't screw into the socket.*
Q: *Could you have had it done over?*
A: *I could have.*
Q: *Then you liked it in fragments and you chose to leave it that way?*
A: *Of course.*

The distinction I try to make between necessity and subjective preference seems unintelligible to Johns. I asked him about the type of numbers and letters he uses — coarse, standardized, unartistic — the type you associate with grocery signs, packing cases, and crates.
Q: *You nearly always use this same type. Any particular reason?*
A: *That's how the stencils come.*
Q: *But if you preferred another type face, would you think it improper to cut your own stencils?*
A: *Of course not.*
Q: *Then you really do like these best?*
A: *Yes.*
This answer is so self-evident that I wonder why I asked the question at all; ah yes — because Johns would not see the obvious distinction between free choice and external necessity. Let me try again:
Q: *Do you use these letter types because you like them or because that's how the stencils come?*
A: *But that's what I like about them, that they come that way.*

Does this mean that it is Johns's choice to prefer the given condition — the shape of commercial stencils, inaccurate workmanship at the foundry, boxes too low to contain plaster masks, etc.? that he so wills what occurs that what comes from without becomes indistinguishable from what he chooses? The theoretic distinction I tried to impose had been fetched from elsewhere; hence its irrelevance.
I had tried to distinguish between letters designed that are subject to expressive inflection, letters that exist in the world of art; and those functional letters that come in mass-produced stencils to spell THIS END UP on a crate. Proceeding by rote from this distinction between life and art, I asked whether the painter entertained an aesthetic preference for these crude stenciled forms.

7

Johns answers that he will not recognize the distinction. He knows that letters of more striking design do exist or can be made to exist. But they would be Art. And what he likes about those stencils is that they are Art not quite yet. He is the realist for whom preformed subject matter is a condition of painting.

4. Johns's subjects are whole entities or complete systems. Either a single thing in its entirety, a figure 5, a target, a shade; or a gamut, a full set, or span of possibilities. The first commonplace object which Johns saw as a picture potentially, was the U.S. flag, whose 13 stripes stand for the sum of the original colonies, and whose stars refer to the full count of states; America then and now. When Johns made bronze sculptures out of two cans of ale, one of them lighter and pierced at the top, was designated as empty, the other as full; one (with the Ballantine sign at the top) was Southern, the other Yankee.

His numbers, when not single images, run zero to nine; his alphabets, A to Z. His *Book* and his *Newspaper* are open to show the full double spread; his *Shade* is wholly unfurled; his *Thermometer* painting calibrates the full scale; and his various circle paintings describe complete revolutions. His most recent large work (about 10 feet wide) is the United States map from coast to coast. All things, whether objects or signs or series, are shown, like Egyptian shoulders, in their longest extension. And the implication here, as in Egyptian art, is the absence of point of view.

As his objects are seen from no particular angle, so there is no intellectual station whence a significant fragment from a larger whole might have been singled out. No partiality. The completeness of his systems or entities implies the artist's refusal to advertise his subjective location.
It is the same with his color. When he is not painting monochromatically, his colors present a schematic abstract of the whole spectrum: Red, Yellow, Blue; or, for greater richness and with a slight turn of the wheel, the intermediate complementaries: Orange, Green, Purple.

But there are the two *Targets* of 1955 (painted when Johns was 25), of which N. Calas once wrote, « Oneness is killed either by repetition or by fragmentation ». One of these displays four truncated life casts of a face painted orange; the other is surmounted by nine boxes whose hinged flaps can be opened and shut, and which contain anatomical fragments in plaster: a near-white face segment, a near-black animal bone, a four-fingered hand painted red, a yellow heel, orange ear, green penis, purple foot and empty blue box. (I should ask Johns why the breast fragment is pink. I did once ask why he had inserted these plaster casts, and his answer was, naturally, that some of the casts happened to be around in the studio).
The fact that these anatomical parts are not whole, that only so much of them is inserted as will fit in each box, that they are clipped to size exactly like bits of collage, indicates that the human body is not the ostensible subject. The subject remains the bull's-eye in its wholeness for which the anatomical fragments provide the emphatic contrast.
Apparently the artist wanted to know whether he could use life casts of the body and no more read them for meaning than he read the linage in the pasted newspaper fragments below. He was exploring a possibility to its limits; and I think he miscalculated. Not in that he failed to make a picture that works, but in that the attitude of detachment required to make it work on his terms is too specialized, too rare, too pitilessly unsentimental, to acquit the work of morbidity. When affective human elements are conspicuously used, and yet not as subjects, their derogation becomes a subject that's got out of control. At any rate, no similar fracturing of known wholes has occurred since in Johns's work.

5. Since they tend to constitute the whole subject of a particular work, **Johns's objects, systems or signs predetermine the picture's shape and dimensions** (*). The picture is not contained by an external frame, but is retained from within. Apollinaire had seen this coming in 1913 when he predicted a greater role in modern art for the real object, which he called the picture's « internal frame ».

In Johns's work the « internal frame » functions obviously wherever a flag, target, alphabet, book, canvas or shade remains self-sufficient. Where an actual object is included in a larger canvas it serves at least to diminish the margin of freedom; the arbitrariness of where the picture ends is reduced.
Thus, in the pictures called *Coat Hanger* and *Drawer*, the lateral span is prefixed, in others, e.g. *Thermometer*, it's the height. In *Gray Painting with Ball* (1958) the

(*) A point observed by Ben Heller: « The subjects limit and describe Johns's space ».

9

height is given by a gash in the canvas, pried and held open by an intruding ball.

In a picture of the following year the subject was to have been a circle. Johns used a flat pivoting stick to trace it, then saw that it would be false to remove it once the tracing was done. The circle alone would have been an abstraction on canvas; with the compass stick in evidence, the picture became an object again: a device for making a circle. The painting's subject, title, and shape suddenly coincided. The circle and the words, DEVICE CIRCLE stenciled across the bottom determine, as if by absolute external necessity, the structure and shape of the work.

One of Johns's most beautiful works is the picture called *Tennyson* (1958), conceived in homage to the poet who had written « The Lotos-Eaters ». The poet's name — for once not stenciled but in Roman capitals — runs across the bottom, setting out the width and even, one feels, the scale of the work. The rest of this large picture (73½ inches high) begins in two tall upright panels on separate stretchers whose junction still shows at the top. Then the painter takes a great length of canvas and lays it down as a folded sheet over the original diptych. For some reason I imagine that I can feel the pace of these simple performances; slow, dark gestures as of an unknown funereal rite. And then the gray brushwork itself overlays the entire field with an all-over falling of grays; and darker grays of gathered density in the letters that spell Tennyson's name.

The important step in this picture was Johns's decision to use no given reality beyond that of the poet's name, but to create, out of invented material geometries, a system equally ineluctible. The physical fashioning of this picture — the separation of the two panels and the folded tapering overlay — these in relation to the paint activity now furnish the pre-conditions of material necessity. An illusion, of course, since these acts of cutting and pasting were themselves free decisions. But their wilfulness operated against another kind of material resistance and implies action earlier in time. At the moment of painting, the system of three visible strata and four fields of canvas was as surely ordained as was, in previous paintings, the design of the American flag.

But what of the arbitrary variations Johns has played on the Stars and Stripes? — the *Flag above White* (1954) or the *Flag on Orange Field* (1957), pictures in which the flag's horizontal design sits incongruously in a tall canvas? It seems to me that the uncanniness of these pictures derives precisely from this, that a visible rule of logic and order and precedent is here visibly broken. When the flag ceases to be all there is; when its perfect

anatomy enters into any kind of combination — it becomes fabulous: a modern realist's counterpart to the chimeras of antique realism.

Take the *Flag above White*: Is the picture unfinished, as if in expectation of more of those horizontal red stripes? This might be good for the picture, but it would ruin the flag.

Does the flag rest on a white base? Impossible since the white of the base and that of the stripes is the same; you can taste it.

But then, is the lower white an excess to be pared away? This might be good for the flag, but it would cut up the picture which is visibly indivisible.

The picture demonstrates its own impossibility. And somewhat the same holds for that younger flag that sits rigid in a vibrating snowdrift of orange.

6. Johns's subjects are flat.

Under an enormous literal representation of an unmistakable pipe Magritte wrote *Ce n'est pas une pipe*. And to the puzzled spectator who mistakes the image for the reality, he would have said — *Try to smoke it*.

Johns's images have not this immunity of the unreal. You can't smoke Magritte's painted pipe, but you can throw a dart at a Johns target, or use his painted alphabets for testing myopia.

If you don't put his targets and letters to use, is it perhaps because you regard them as art? But that's your decision. You are free to spare his targets, or anyone's targets; for, as we said before, Johns renders visible the possibility of an alternative attitude. The point is, however, that it is an alternative; that the posture of aiming at a Johns target is no less sane than was genuflection before a mosaic saint. Because the subject in Johns's art has regained real presence.

In his home-grown morality, wherein it is unethical to turn things away from themselves, a painting must be what it represents. Paint is paint, and numbers are numbers, and you can have a painted number in which each term is only itself. You can also have objects with paint on them. What you cannot have is a painted landscape, where the landscape is counterfeit and the paint is disguised.

Was it, I wonder, a painful decision, that paint was to be no longer a medium of transformation? Probably not; for the painter it must have been merely the taking of the next step. But once taken, it placed him at a point outside the crowded room, whence one suddenly saw

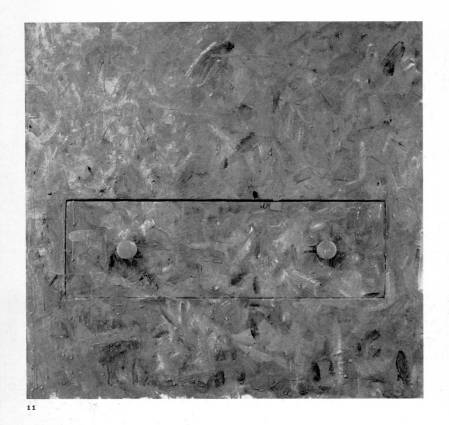

11

12

how Franz Kline bundles with Watteau and Giotto. For they are all artists who use paint and surface to suggest existences other than surface and paint.

The degree of non-figurative abstraction has nothing to do with it. Existences other than those of paint are implied when dark nearing blacks block the openness of a white space; when pure color patches are allowed to locate themselves at varying distances from the picture plane; when painted canvas permits the illusion that form and space, figure and ground are not of one stuff. Johns eliminates a residue of double dealing in modern painting. Since his picture plane is to be flat, nothing is paintable without make-believe but what is flat by nature. And if for some reason he wants something 3-D, let the artist insert the thing, or a cast of it.

Does all this mean that Johns is a respecter of « the integrity of the picture plane ? ».
On the contrary. He is that sovereign painter who respects it so little that he is willing to let his subjects take care of the matter.

Have you noticed how his paint is laid on? The brush-strokes don't blend; each makes its short shape, distinct in tone from its neighbor. This is the way Cézanne used to paint, in broken planes composed of adjacent values; imparting pictorial flatness to things which the mind knows to be atmospheric and spatial. Johns, with that same type of brushwork that hovers midway between opaque canvas and spatial illusion, does the reverse: allowing an atmospheric suggestion to things which the mind knows to be flat. In fact, he relies on his subject matter to find and retain the picture plane for him, leaving him free to work, as he put it, *on other levels.*

Not for a generation has subject matter been of such radical formal importance as in his recent *Map* (1961). We are used, in reading maps, to seeing blue waters against earth-colored land. But Johns's picture disperses Blue, Yellow, Red and some new derivatives in even quantities all over the map. If this were anything but a map — a quilt of pure color relations — the blues that now ride most of Texas and Iowa would recede unfathomably. Johns counts on our knowledge that this is a map to maintain surface tension against the natural spatial pressures of color; just as Poussin, when he drapes a girl's skiey thigh in the foreground in blue, counts on our understanding of foregrounds and thighs to hold the recessive color in place.

Is it not now apparent how far from arbitrary, how far from the spirit of Dada, from any desire to provoke some uncaring bourgeois Johns is in the choice of his themes?

13

14

Look at the flag again, the first of his found subjects and, in its natural state, almost a preformed Johnsian system. The red and white stripes do not — as in a normal striped pattern — form a figure-ground hierarchy. They are, in their familiar symbolic role, absolutely equivalent. In other words, the alternation of red and white stripes in the American flag is much flatter than similar stripes on a T-shirt would be. As for the stars on blue ground, here, as in all situations that threaten a figure-ground differential, Johns employs all his techniques as a painter to cancel the difference. Among others:

A. The ceaseless overlap-interlace of figure and ground; the paint surface, as in knitting or basketry. Not a shallow space but the quickened density of a film.
B. An M-W brushstroke that looks and functions somewhat like the corrugated staples carpenters use.
C. The unpainted lower edge of most of his canvases.
D. The drip, familiar hallmark of New York School painting, acting like loosed raindrops when they tie up a whole (not previously visible) window pane. Look for it in the *Map* — and how restful to be able to specify where: e.g. the drips that trickle from the Dakotas down into Nebraska, and the red skeins where New York overflows to the south.
E. Collage fragments, newspaper or a patch of fresh canvas, to recall the painting to materiality wherever color

or tone values overreach into illusory space. It is something like a *memento mori*: Remember, the picture is told, thy flat abject nature.

I keep looking at his black-and-white painting called *Shade*, done in 1959. But for a narrow margin all around, its entire surface is taken up by a window shade, the kind you buy for $ 2.95 at department stores, pulled down as if for the night; this one obviously for the last time. Over all the available surface, shade and ground-canvas alike, spreads the painting itself, suggesting a cavernous nocturnal space with bursts in it of white lights, that radiate from indeterminate points, like bursting and falling fireworks misted over.
An abstracted landscape? You stare at and into a field whose darkness is absolute, whose whites brighten nothing, but make darkness visible, as Milton said of infernal shade.
Or a scene of nightfall: far lights flare and fade, move into focus and out, like rainy lights from a highway. Are we out inside the night, or indoors? A window is within reach, and its shade (standard variety available at discount houses for $ 1.95) is pulled down. Shutting us out; or, to judge from the shade's tenacity, closing us in.
On a shade of flat canvas drawn against the outside he shows outdoor darkness; like the dark space known to

closed eyes. And are eyelids lowered like windowshades against outer light comparable to picture planes? Alberti compared the open paintings he knew to windows. « Shade » compares a (now-painted) canvas to a window whose plain canvas shade — to be had like ours, secondhand for a dollar — is down.

7. Johns's subjects are non-hierarchic. When Johns paints in color his effort is to maintain each of the colors in a state of allover dispersion and in similar quantities. There is to be no predominance.

When he paints figures, such as numbers or letters, the negative spaces are given just enough occasional overlap to cancel the hierarchic distinction between figure and ground.

The objects he incorporates in his pictures are those that are equally uninteresting to tramp and tycoon.

Actual instruments of differentiation (e.g. inserted rulers, thermometers) can but interrupt the painting — whose homogeneity cannot acknowledge their calibrations.

Within Johns's pictorial fields, all the members exist in a state of democratic equality, every part of the image tending towards the picture plane, as water tends to sea level. The paint surface, waved and incidented but leveled and leveling like the surface of water; and one imagines that any part could replace any other at any point. No part of the picture swells at the expense of another; whence the prominence in Johns's work of the U.S. flag, the most egalitarian composition ever conceived.

In other words, no one is pointing at anything in particular, perhaps because no one's around.

What of the Targets, however? As objects of use they are designed to feature one center; they represent total convergence upon a privileged point. But Johns's treatment of targets neutralizes their natural centripetal stress, chiefly by the strong decentralized red in the spandrels. And it must have been partly in order to offset the look of centralization that Johns burdened two of his targets with boxed anatomical casts. They form an aimless procession to and fro on a shelved horizontal, and invite the vertical up-and-down motion of raising and closing the flaps. One good reason for their inclusion was surely the determination to bring this most centralizing of all possible forms down to a state of homogeneous de-emphasis. Hence also his target paintings that are all-green and all-white. Johns unfocuses even the target so that, being seen not with a marksman's eye, it is seen with an alternative attitude; or with none.

It is characteristic of Johns that having by certain means achieved a certain desired appearance, he goes on to see whether he may not get the same result by the opposite means: whether he can make a target look as decentralized as a flag; whether he can make the upright *Flag Above White* look as indivisible as a flag alone; and, in his two targets with plaster casts, whether the effect of randomness, procured by anatomical fragments from all over the body, can be attained also by a fourfold repetition of the same single face; and whether male privates in plaster may be made to seem as indifferently public as the cast of a hand; and whether, having aroused the spectator's sense of participation by means of hinged flaps which he can open at will, the spectator may not be stirred to the same sense of participation by means of a drawer which remains shut.

Moral: Nothing in art is so true that its opposite cannot be made even truer.

8. Johns's subjects are associable with sufferance rather than action.

All objects are passive, and Johns's paintings are objects. But objects get themselves associated with specific actions and, accordingly, with degrees of doing and suffering. A flag has nothing to do but be recognized; a target is aimed at; letters and numbers are shuffled, and drawers are opened and filled. Even the hook Johns has drawn extends no prehensile claw, but curls up to a *retroussé* point.

Abetted by his manner of painting, his subjects tend to create areas of uneventful endurance; the subjects themselves yielding patterns of humdrum continuity that simply abide under the erosive activity of the paint. It seems to hold for the early work. Then, by 1958, Johns introduced elements of assertive action into his pictures which became readable as polarities of doing and suffering. Things that acted and things acted upon appeared in conjunction. In the *Gray Painting with Ball* (1958) the ball works as a forceful intrusion, a foreign body within the gashed canvas. The pivoting stick that remained behind in *Device Circle* (1959) is an efficient agent that makes its mark wherever it touches.

Such changes are worth pointing to since they indicate that Johns's language of objects is wide open to life.

His subject matter is the sensitive, obedient vehicle of his intentions as person and painter. It is not there in default of some more intriguing topic, nor to beard innocent Babbitts into a rage of incomprehension. His themes were not chosen to refine our blunt sensibilities, nor indeed for any reason having to do with you and me. Johns chose his particular subjects because they were the ones that best permitted him to live his painter's life. That is to say, they alone would convey him and his hand — in the way they both wished to be traveling — from edge to edge of the day's canvas.

painting with two balls. 1960 j. johns

26

16

WHAT IS A PAINTING?

You don't just ask; you advance a hypothesis.
The question is, What is a Picture? or What sort of presence is the Picture Plane? And the hypothesis takes the form of a painting.

It is part of the fascination of Johns's work that many of his inventions are interpretable as meditations on the nature of painting, pursued as if in a dialogue with a questioner of ideal innocence and congenital blindness. *A picture, you see, is a piece of canvas nailed to a stretcher. Like this?* says the blindman, holding it up with its face to the wall. Then Johns makes a picture of that kind of picture to see whether it will make a picture. Or: *A picture is what a painter puts whatever he has into. You mean like a drawer? Not quite; remember it's flat. Like the front of a drawer?* The thought takes form as a picture — and don't let's ask whether this is what the artist had thought while he made it. It's what the picture gives you to think that counts.
If pictures are flat, said the blindman, *why do they always speak of things IN pictures? Why, what's wrong with it? Things ON pictures, it should be; like things on trays or on walls. That's right. Well then, when something is IN a picture, where is it? Behind the canvas, like a concealed music box?* (Cf. Johns's *Tango*, 1955).

What would happen if you dropped one of Cézanne's apples into a Still Life by Renoir? Would the weight of it sink it right through the table? Would the table itself pulverize like disturbed dust or down from a torn pillow? Yet this is the standard anomaly of conceiving an alien solid quartered upon or within a pictorial field. The blindman refused to believe that it could be done. *Show me*, he said; and Johns painted *Gray Painting with Ball*. He has worked valiantly to keep this blindman inform-ed, him who believes nothing that he cannot touch. *Green Target* was a special donation; a target in Braille, so to speak.
And the logic of it is overwhelming. If a painting is truly an object; — repeat: if that which is painted is truly an object — then that which is painted cannot be a pure-ly optic phenomenon. It must possess visible tangibi-lity. And in that case any painting can be rehearsed with either its visual or its tactual modality played up or played down. A painting of Johns may be flattened into a draw-ing, or relieved in sculpmetal and bronze. A drawing (which Johns usually makes *after* a painting) abstracts from the picture its visibility. Green targets, bleached and bronze flags, all tricolor emblems reduced to texture alone, approach pure palpability.

Among Johns's most recent paintings, and in the same group with *LIAR*, is a larger picture called *NO*. Its painted field is made up of soft mottled grays. Fastened to a hook near the top, is a long unshaped wire that hangs loose and free. From its lower end dangle the letters NO in aluminum foil, casting a vagrant shadow. The shadow writes NO again near a place that's al-ready big with the same message — the word NO raised on the canvas in sculpmetal relief.
Both this picture and *LIAR* seem to me to write a new role for the picture plane: not a window, nor an up-righted tray, nor yet an object with active projections in actual space; but a surface observed during impregna-tion, as it receives a message or imprint from real space.

A good modern picture plane that lets forms project out in space (always crossing the line between art and life!) can perhaps be prefabricated. What you need is a solid protrusion that you can hang anything on — like a knob and an empty coat hanger; or a pair of hooks in the surface. They make picture planes of enormous po-tential. And in the latter case, the picture plane becomes real enough to be presentable in side elevation.

Johns has painted and drawn a series of pictures which he called *Zero through Nine*. Not « Zero *to* Nine », like the handsome white painting of the previous year; but « through » — to intimate that procession had given way to transparency and superposition. As if the pro-gression of cardinal numbers had suddenly become faintly improper for implying a prearranged motion from left to right, setting up a pecking order from first to last. It accords well with his moral position that Johns should have hit on the idea of annulling the seniority rule among numbers. Now all the ten cyphers, drawn to one scale, are superimposed in one place.

17

18

19

20

21

But « superimposed » is the wrong word; it suggests stratification. And the point about these numbers is that they coexist simultaneously in the same level.

But « same » too is the wrong word. The same river cannot be stepped into twice, and just so, no cypher here steps into the same situation, since each entering form alters it for the next, while changing the place for all previous tenants.

What sort of a place is this that can hold ten simultaneous presences in solution? Is it anything like that head of a pin that supports a number of angels? Or a movie screen with a memory?...

Some years ago Johns was asked at a party what he would do if he were not a painter. He said he would run a lending collection of paintings to tour the country by air. The distributing aircraft, he said, would be labeled: « The Picture Plane ».

HOW IMPROPER IS IT TO FIND POETIC, METAPHORICAL OR EMOTIONAL CONTENT IN JOHNS'S WORK?

I remember how, four years ago, my initial dismay over Johns's work was overcome by the pictures themselves. A suspicion of their destructive or unserious intention was dissipated not only by their commanding presence and workmanlike quality, but by something that impressed me as the intensity of their solitude. And this despite their deadpan materiality, and despite the artist's assurance that no emotional content was either overtly or implicitly present. When I said to him recently that his early works seemed to me to be « about human absence », he replied that this would mean their failure for him; for it would imply « that he had been there », whereas he wants his pictures to be objects alone.

Well then I think he fails; not as a painter, but as theorist. For the assumption of a realism of absolute impersonality always does fail — if taken too seriously. That assumption is itself a way of feeling; it is the ascetic passion which sustains the youthful drive of a Caravaggio, Vélazquez, or Courbet while they shake the emotional slop from themselves and their models.

Johns's earliest surviving picture — for he destroyed many — has a romantic melancholy about it, even a hint of self-pity. It is the lovely small *Construction with*

Piano, 1954. Compared with such a piece, the symbolism of his recent gray paintings — *LIAR*, *NO*, *Good Time Charley*, *In Memory of my Feelings* — is both more overt and more impenetrable. The painter past 30 dares to be frankly autobiographical because his sense of self is objectified, and because he feels secure in the strength of his artistic language.

Between that early covert lament and these latest tough-minded personal symbols, lie the paintings I have chiefly discussed, works that were to have been of the most uncompromising impersonal objectivity.

Target with 4 Faces (1955) was to have been just that and no more — without content, if content implied the artist in attendance pumping it in. But that's not what's implied at all. The content in Johns's work gives the impression of being self-generated — so potent are his juxtapositions.

Here in this work the rigid stare of the bull's-eye is surmounted by four eyeless life casts of one face. Suppose the juxtaposition was performed without any expressive intent. Then, within the worldframe of this picture, the values that would make a face seem more eloquent or remarkable than a target are not being held anymore. And this is not a logical deduction, but refers to something one sees.

But the things one knows also enter in. Thus the target appears in its known true colors; but the face is orange all over. The target is whole; but the face is cut down. The target, of which one tends to have many, is single; the face, of which one has one alone, has been multiplied. In common experience, targets are known at a distance; but a target that cannot be missed has lost its identity, just like a 4-times-repeated face on a shelf. So then, if the target and the facial casts had no correlative meaning when the artist first put them together, the life they now lead in his picture gives them a common constraint. They seem to have traded their respective stakes in space. For the target that belongs at a distance, « out there », has acquired absolute « hereness ». And the human face, which is experienced as « here », has been dismissed to « up there ». As if the subjective space consciousness that gives meaning to the words « here » and « there » had ceased operation.

And then I saw that Johns's pictures, in the passivity of their subjects and their slow lasting through time, tend to convey a sense of perpetual waiting — like the canvas face-to-the-wall that waits to be turned, or the empty coat hanger. But it is a waiting for nothing, since the objects as Johns presents them, acknowledge no living presence; they imply human absence from a man-made environment. Only man's objects remain, overgrown by paint as by indifferent vegetation. Familiar objects, but Johns has anticipated their dereliction.

23

And is this finally what the picture means?

No, not that at all. Who would need pictures if they were that translatable? What I am trying to say is that Johns can put two things in a picture and make them work against one another so hard that nothing seems too far-fetched to account for the shock received.

I conclude with a few suggestions for criticizing what I have written:
Too much reading in of subjective interpretations.
The author proceeds from the naive assumption that art is reducible to concepts and ideas.
Nothing that he has said has any bearing on Johns's painting *qua* painting.
He treats Jasper Johns in complete isolation, as if nobody else were painting at all!

24

25

26

27

28

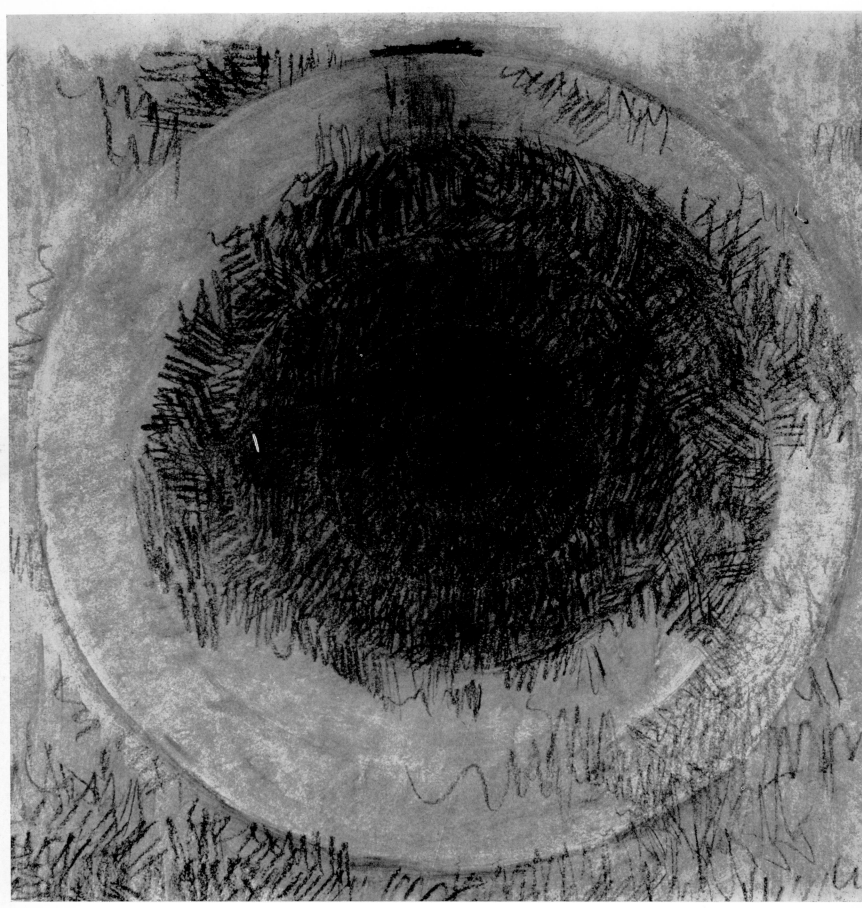

29

30

32

41

Illustrations

33

Bibliography   *by James P. Hardy*

BOOKS

DORFLES, GILLO. *Ultime tendenze nell'arte d'oggi.* p. 169. Feltrinelli. Milan. 1961

FRIEDMAN, B. H., ed. *School of New York: Some Younger Artists.* « Jasper Johns » (Ben Heller). pp. 30-35. Grove Press Inc. NYC. 1959.

JANIS, HARRIET & BLESH, RUDI. *Collage.* p. 246. Chilton Co. NYC. Philadelphia 1962

MILLER, DOROTHY, ed. *Sixteen Americans.* pp. 22-27. Museum of Modern Art. NYC. 1959

SEITZ, WILLIAM. *The Art of Assemblage.* p. 74. Museum of Modern Art. NYC. 1961

SEUPHOR, MICHEL. *Abstract Painting.* p. 306. Abrams. NYC. 1962

VIVALDI, CAESARE, ed. *Almanacco Letterario Bompiani.* p. 255. Milan. 1962

PERIODICALS

Rosenblum, Robert. *Arts*, May, 1957 (gallery group at Leo Castelli)

Porter, Fairfield. *Art News*, Jan., 1958 (exhibition at Leo Castelli; cover)

Rosenblum, Robert. *Arts*, Jan., 1958 (exhibition at Leo Castelli)

Preston, Stuart. *New York Times*, Jan., 1958 (exhibition at Leo Castelli)

Newsweek, 31 Mar., 1958 « Targets and Flags »

Washburn, G. B. *Carnegie Magazine*, Dec., 1958 « Pittsburgh Bicentennial International: the Prize Awards »

Ragon, Michel. *Cimaise*, Jan.-Feb.-Mar., 1959 « Art today in the United States »

Mademoiselle, Jan., 1959 (illustration)

Calas, Nicolas. *Art News*, Feb., 1959 « ContiNuance »

Kramer, Hilton. *Arts*, Feb., 1959 « Art and the Found Object »

Apollo, Mar., 1959 (exhibition at Galerie Rive Droite)

Schneider, Pierre. *Art News*, Mar., 1959 (exhibition at Galerie Rive Droite)

Arts, Mar., 1959 (Letters)

44 *Charm*, Apr., 1959 « Five Young Artists »

Time, 4 May, 1959 « His heart belongs to Dada »

Ashton, Dore. *New York Times*, May, 1959 « Five Temperaments »

Preston, Stuart. *New York Times*, 25 Oct., 1959 (« Work in Three Dimensions » at Leo Castelli)

Tillim, Sidney. *Arts*, Dec., 1959 (« Work in Three Dimensions » at Leo Castelli)

Genauer, Emily. *New York Herald Tribune*, 16 Dec., 1959 (« Sixteen Americans »)

Preston, Stuart. *New York Times*, 16 Dec., 1959 (« Sixteen Americans »)

Coates, Robert. *New Yorker*, 2 Jan., 1960 « Sixteen Americans »

Rubin, William. *Art International* IV/1, 1960 « Younger American Painters »

Sandler, I. H. *Art News*, Feb., 1960 (exhibition at Leo Castelli)

Genauer, Emily. *New York Herald Tribune*, 21 Feb., 1960 (exhibition at Leo Castelli)

Judd, Donald. *Arts*, Mar., 1960 (exhibition at Leo Castelli)

Tono, Yoshiaki. *Mizue*, Mar., 1960 « New Adventures in American Art »

Porter, Fairfield. *Nation*, 19 Mar., 1960 (exhibition at Leo Castelli)

Myers, John B. *Evergreen Review*, Mar.-Apr. 1960 « The Impact of Surrealism on the New York School »

Genauer, Emily. *New York Herald Tribune*, 3 Apr., 1960 (exhibition at Leo Castelli)

S., J. K. *Minneapolis Tribune*, 15 May, 1960 (exhibition at Tweed Gallery)

Tono, Yoshiaki. *Art in America*, Summer, 1960 « From a Gulliver's Point of View »

Life, 19 Sept., 1960 « Fine Arts in the Market Place »

Rosenblum, Robert. *Art International* IV/7, Sept., 1960 « Jasper Johns »

Dick, D. R. *The State Magazine* Columbia, S. C., 15 Jan., 1961 « Art's Fair-Haired Boy »

Preston, Stuart. *New York Times*, 12 Feb., 1961 (drawings, sculpture and lithographs at Leo Castelli)

Burroughs, Carlyle. *New York Herald Tribune*, 12 Feb., 1961 (drawings, sculpture and lithographs at Leo Castelli)

Tillim, Sidney. *Arts*, Mar., 1961 (drawings, sculpture and lithographs at Leo Castelli)

Sandler, I. H. *Art News*, Mar., 1961 (drawings, sculpture and lithographs at Leo Castelli)

Sandler, I. H. *Art International* V/3, 1961 « New York Letter »

New York Herald Tribune, European Edition, 28 June, 1961 (exhibition at Galerie Rive Droite)

Restany, Pierre. *Cimaise*, Sept., 1961 « Jasper Johns and the Metaphysic of the Commonplace »

Ashbery, John. *Art International* V/8, Oct., 1961 (exhibition at Galerie Rive Droite)

Hess, Thomas. *Art News*, Nov., 1961 « Collage as an Historical Method »

Schuyler, James. *Art News*, Jan., 1962 « Is There an American Print Revival ? »

Domus, Jan., 1962 (Carnegie International exhibition at Pittsburgh)

Tillim, Sidney. *Playboy*, Jan., 1962 « The Fine Art of Acquiring Fine Art »

Rosenblum, Robert. *XXe Siècle*, Feb., 1962 « Oeuvres recentes de Jasper Johns »

Steinberg, Leo. *Harper's*, Mar., 1962 « Contemporary Art and the Plight of Its Public »

Linde, Ulf. *Dagens Nyheter*, Stockholm, 17 Mar., 1962 « 4 Amerikanare »

Svenska Dagbladet Stockholm, 17 Mar., 1962 « 4 Amerikanare »

Edlund, Hans. *Aftonbladet*, Stockholm, 17 Mar., 1962 « 4 Americakanare Torpederar det Gamla Konstverket »

Brunius, Clas. *Expressen*, Stockholm, 17 Mar., 1962 « 4 Amerikanare »

Dagens Nyheter, Stockholm, 18 Mar., 1962 « 4 Amerikanare »

Bailey, Suzanne. *Ameryka* ‡ 34 (U.S. Information Agency, Polish edition), Spring, 1962 « Four Young Artists »

O'Hara, Frank. *Kulchur* 5, Spring, 1962 « Art Chronicle »

Tono, Yoshiaki. *Mizue*, Apr., 1962 « Jasper Johns or the Metaphysics of Vulgarity »

SELECTED EXHIBITION CATALOGUES

Artists of the New York School: Second Generation. The Jewish Museum. New York, 1957

Collage International. Contemporary Arts Museum. Houston, 1958

XXIX Biennale. Venice, 1958

A Decade of Contemporary Drawings. Contemporary Arts Museum. Houston, 1958

The 1958 Pittsburgh Bicentennial International Exhibition of Contemporary Painting and Sculpture. Carnegie Institute. Pittsburgh, 1958

Collage in America. Zabriskie Gallery, and American Federation of Arts. New York, 1958

100 American Works on Paper. Boston Institute of Contemporary Art. Boston, 1959

Graphik der Gegenwart. Galerie Kunst der Gegenwart. Salzburg, 1959

Out of the Ordinary. The Contemporary Arts Association. Houston, 1959

Contemporary American Painting. Whitney Museum of American Art. New York, 1959

Exposition inteRnatiOnale du Surréalisme. Galerie Daniel Cordier. Paris, 1959

Contemporary American Painting. Columbus Museum of Art. Columbus, Ohio, 1960

New Media - New Forms I. Martha Jackson Gallery. New York, 1960

Annual Exhibition 1960 Contemporary American Sculpture and Drawings. Whitney Museum of American Art. New York, 1960

64th American Exhibition - Paintings, Sculpture. The Art Institute of Chicago. Chicago, 1961

The VI Tokyo Biennale. Tokyo Metropolitan Art Gallery. Tokyo, 1961

The Pittsburgh International Exhibition of Contemporary Painting and Sculpture. Carnegie Institute. Pittsburgh, 1961

Bewogen Beweging. Stedelijk Museum. Amsterdam, 1961

Rorelse I Konsten. Moderna Museet. Stockholm, 1961

Le Nouveau Réalisme à Paris et à New York. Galerie Rive Droite. Paris, 1961

American Abstract Expressionists and Imagists. Guggenheim Museum. New York, 1961

Contemporary American Painting. Whitney Museum of American Art. New York, 1961

American Vanguard. (United States Information Agency). Shown at Vienna, Salzburg, six cities in Yugoslavia, London and Darmstadt. 1961-62

Abstract Drawings and Watercolors: U.S.A. (International Council of the Museum of Modern Art, New York). Shown in 7 Latin American countries, 1961-1963

65th Annual American Exhibition. The Art Institute of Chicago. Chicago, 1962

The Maremont Collection at the Institute of Design. Illinois Institute of Technology. Chicago, 1962

Art Since 1950. Seattle World's Fair. Seattle, 1962

Dessins Americains Contemporains. (International Council of the Museum of Modern Art, New York). Centre Culturel Americain. Paris, 1962

Amerikanische Zeichnungen. (International Council of the Museum of Modern Art, New York). Stadtische Kunstsammlungen. Bonn, 1962

Jasper Johns Retrospective Exhibition. Everett Ellin Galle y. Los Angeles, 1962

Major exhibitions

This list includes one-man shows, marked with *, and other exhibitions in which three works or more were displayed

1958   *New York.* Leo Castelli Gallery*. 20 Jan.-8 Feb.

      Newport. R. I. Cushing Memorial Gallery. Jazz Festival Exhibition. 1 July-31 July

      Venice. 29th Biennale. 14 June-30 Sept.

1959   *Paris.* Galerie Rive Droite*. Opening 16 Jan.

      Milan. Galleria d'Arte del Naviglio*. Opening 21 Mar.

      New York. Museum of Modern Art. Sixteen Americans. 16 Dec. - 14 Feb. 1960

1960   *New York.* Leo Castelli Gallery*. 15 Feb.-5 Mar.

      Minneapolis, Minn. Tweed Gallery, University of Minneapolis*. 3 May-15 June

      Los Angeles. Ferus Gallery. Jasper Johns-Kurt Schwitters. 6 Sept.-30 Sept.

      Columbia. S. C. The Columbia Museum of Art*. 7 Dec.-29 Dec.

1961   *New York.* Leo Castelli Gallery*. 31 Jan.-25 Feb.

      Paris. Galerie Rive Droite*. 13 June-12 July

      U.S.I.A. American Vanguard Exhibition. *Vienna,* 19 June-8 July; *Salzburg,* 10 July-31 Aug.; *Belgrade, Skoplje, Zagreb, Maribor, Ljubljana, Rijeka,* 15 Sept.-31 Jan. 1962; *London,* U.S.I.S. Gallery, American Embassy, 28 Feb.-30 Mar. 1962; *Darmstadt,* Landesmuseum, 14 Apr.-13 May 1962

      New York. Kornblee Gallery. The Fine Art of Lithography. 28 Nov.-30 Dec.

1962   *Stockholm.* Moderna Museet. 4 Amerikanare. 17 Mar.-6 May.

      Amsterdam. Stedelijk Museum. 4 Amerikanen. Opening 18 June.

      Bern. Kunsthalle. 4 Amerikaner. 7 July - 22 Sept.

      Los Angeles. Everett Ellin Gallery*. 19 Nov. - 15 Dec.

      Paris. Ileana Sonnabend Galerie*. 15 Nov. - 31 Dec.

Biographical data

Jasper Johns was born in Allendale, South Carolina, May 15, 1930. He studied at the University of South Carolina briefly, and came to New York in 1952, He lives in New York and Edisto Beach, South Carolina,

Photographic credits

Eric Pollitzer: cover

Rudolph Burckhardt: 1, 2, 3, 4, 6, 9, 10, 11, 13, 14, 15, 16, 17, 19, 20, 21, 22, 23, 24, 25, 26, 27, 28, 29, 30, 31, 32, 33

Ed Meneeley: 5, 7, 8, 12, 18.